GUIDED JOURNAL

Simple & Free

GUIDED JOURNAL

JEN HATMAKER

CONVERGENT
NEW YORK

THIS JOURNAL BELONGS TO:

_____

Dear Reader,

I am delighted you are here. Welcome to the *Simple & Free* experiment (formerly known as the *7* experiment).

Simple & Free is not a template. It is not a list of rules. It is not a program. It is simply an imperfect social experiment to help us find God in an overcrowded, overindulged, overscheduled life. If any word, any sentence, any section you read helps you cut through the chaos and simplify down to something meaningful, I will count it nothing but a privilege that I was able to walk alongside you in some small way. This has absolutely nothing to do with rules or guilt and everything to do with freedom. Much, much love to you, dear reader.

Love,

Jen

This weirdo little life you are constructing? Where you follow Jesus to strange places, take risks, and do bizarre things? It's all worth it. Every day of it. It only gets more exciting and meaningful. When God asks you to do something, do it. He is such a trustworthy leader. Don't be afraid. You've put your chips all in on the right number.

INTRO

Welcome to a little social experiment that changed our lives for good. I can say that now, because although this specific season is in my rearview mirror, as I looked back through every word I jotted down during my first foray into this experiment, I was surprised how many ideas were so new to me then, because they are the air we breathe today.

Let that be good news to you: No matter if anything you encounter in these next seven months seems too hard or crazy or overwhelming, maybe it will just be Step One into a new idea. Maybe in seven weeks, seven months, or seven years, you'll discover yourself embedded within an entirely new way of life; you won't even remember not thinking that way.

Remember, we're jumping into the *Simple & Free* experiment together. Some of us are brand-new, some are trying again, some of us are still living out the elements we learned from our experiment years ago. But we're all a part of this journey. We're all committed to being lifelong learners who are less attached to certainty and Being Right, and more interested in paying attention and developing.

Let's begin.

CONTENTS

MONTH ONE

FOOD

Picking seven foods is like trying to pick my favorite kid . . . so clearly this category required some thought. After consulting those who know me best, and after much, much prayer, I landed on these guys: chicken, eggs, whole-wheat bread, sweet potatoes, spinach, avocados, and apples.

Month one, day one—time to choose the seven simple foods we'll eat for the next thirty days. As you determine your choices, keep in mind the purpose of *Simple & Free*: to embark on a journey of less. To purge the excessive mess of choice and pare down to what is necessary. It's an exercise in simplicity—not a pursuit of the latest that diet culture has to offer.

DAY 1

What seven foods will you choose for this month?

1.

2.

3.

4.

5.

6.

7.

DAY 2

What's your motivation for embarking on this journey? What is the quiet hope you have for this experiment? Write it all down here—the more specific, the more helpful these words will be for you in those moments when this journey starts to lose its sexiness. Our reasons for starting this experiment can only help in the road ahead. What are yours?

DAY 3

Who are the people with you
on this journey? They could be
friends or family members with
whom you've talked about this
journey, or they could be
coworkers or church groups
who are coming along for the
ride. Who are those folks in
your corner, and what makes
them safe people for you?

_____

_____

_____

_____

_____

_____

_____

_____

_____

_____

_____

_____

_____

_____

_____

DAY 4

What are some words that have
been nourishing for you lately?
They could be lyrics from a
song; they could be Scripture;
they could be poems. They
could be quotes by Michael
Pollan or Ruth Reichl or Chrissy
Teigen—or any writer for that
matter. Write some of those
lines here.

DAY 5

Dear Coffee: I miss you already. We're just on a break. Don't worry. They say if you love something, set it free; and if it comes back to you, then it was truly addicted to you in the first place. Hold on to that. Mark it down: Jen/Java reunion in twenty-five days. Be strong.

DAY 6

What are some ways you can pursue creativity? They could be big or small. They could be trying out a new recipe that uses your foods. They could be making up a recipe yourself! Brainstorm, imagine—or even just jot down ways you've already been mixing things up.

DAY 7

All right. Seven days in. Be
honest: What do you hate the
most about this?

_____

_____

_____

_____

_____

_____

_____

_____

_____

_____

_____

_____

_____

_____

_____

DAY 8

What are some of your favorite
meals? Why? Do they remind
you of home? What memories
arise when you think of these
meals?

DAY 9

This is a fast, a major reduction of the endless possibilities that accompany my every meal. It is supposed to be uncomfortable and inconvenient. This shake-up of my routine commands my attention. I can no longer default to normal, usual, mindless, thoughtless. It's like having an eyelash under my contact all day. What will the Spirit do with this new space? We'll see.

DAY 10

What in my life, if taken away, would alter my value or identity?

DAY 11

What causes an unhealthy
change of attitude, personality,
or focus when "it" becomes
threatened?

DAY 12

Brace yourself for a tsunami of convictions here. What is the thing outside of God that you put everything else on hold for?

After the shine
wears off, the real
spiritual work
begins.

DAY 14

What do you want more of in
your life? What do you want to
shed?

DAY 15

Here's something I prayed in the thick of my first *Simple & Free* experiment: "Jesus, please help me find gratitude. This whole thing feels stupid." Write out your own prayer for today.

DAY 16

Describe the way you were raised to think about food.

_____

_____

_____

_____

_____

_____

_____

_____

_____

_____

_____

_____

_____

_____

_____

_____

Teaching by example, radical obedience, justice, mercy, activism, and sacrifice wholly inspire me. . . . I'm at that place where "well done" trumps "well said." The careful study of the Word has a goal, which is not the careful study of the Word. The objective is to discover Jesus and allow Him to <u>change our trajectory</u>.

DAY 18

List five ways you plan to find rest, fun, and nourishment this week.

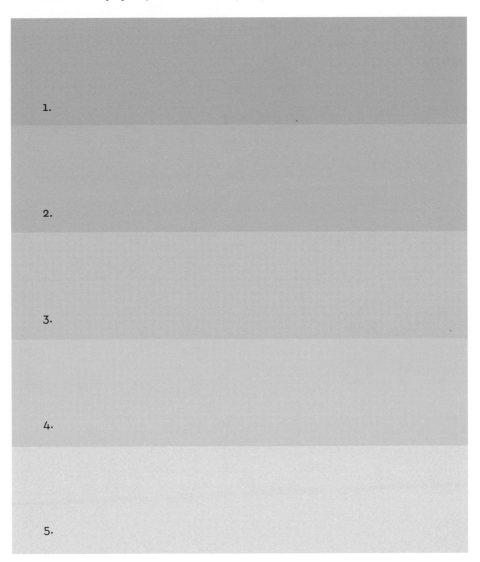

1.

2.

3.

4.

5.

DAY 19

What are some conceptions of
Jesus you've learned to shed
over your life? What are some
new ways you're pursuing the
way of Jesus lately?

_____

_____

_____

_____

_____

_____

_____

_____

_____

_____

_____

_____

_____

_____

_____

DAY 20

In your pursuit of shedding and simplifying your life in the past twenty days, what are some things you feel like you've gained? They could be new insights, observations, or affirmations. Anything.

_____

_____

_____

_____

_____

_____

_____

_____

_____

_____

_____

_____

_____

_____

_____

_____

DAY 21

In so many ways I am the opposite of Jesus' lifestyle. This keeps me up at night. I can't have authentic communion with Him while mired in the trappings He begged me to avoid. . . . But we can forge a small sense of solidarity with Jesus: Blessed are the meek. Humble yourself like a child. Sell all your things and give to the poor. Don't gain the world only to forfeit your soul.

DAY 22

What do you feel excited for?

_____

_____

_____

_____

_____

_____

_____

_____

_____

_____

_____

_____

_____

_____

_____

_____

DAY 23

In the words of Barbara Brown
Taylor (and me), what is saving
your life right now?

_____

_____

_____

_____

_____

_____

_____

_____

_____

_____

_____

_____

_____

_____

_____

_____

DAY 24

In the absence of endless choices, where are you finding the fulfill-ment you might otherwise find in an abundance of food options?

DAY 25

There are days when we seek
   things for ourselves
and measure failure by what we
   do not gain.
On the Sabbath we seek not to
   acquire but to share.
There are days when we exploit
   nature
as if it were a horn of plenty that
   can never be exhausted.
On the Sabbath we stand in
   wonder before the mystery of
   creation.
There are days when we act as if
   we cared nothing for the rights
   of others.
On the Sabbath we are reminded
   that justice is our duty and a
   better world our goal.
Therefore we welcome Shabbat.
Day of rest, day of wonder, day of
   peace.
                    —Shabbat reading

DAY 26

What has surprised you during this first month?

_____

_____

_____

_____

_____

_____

_____

_____

_____

_____

_____

_____

_____

_____

_____

_____

_____

_____

_____

DAY 27

What are you grateful for today?

_____

_____

_____

_____

_____

_____

_____

_____

_____

_____

_____

_____

_____

_____

_____

DAY 28

On the way to contemplation we do
the same thing that Jesus Christ did in
the wilderness. Jesus teaches us not to
say, "Lord, Lord," but to do the will of
his Father. What must primarily con-
cern us is that we do what Jesus has
bidden us do. Jesus went into the wilderness, ate nothing for forty days,
and made himself empty. . . . Of course,
emptiness in and of itself isn't enough.
The point of emptiness is to get ourselves out of the way so that Christ
can fill us up. As soon as we're empty,
there's a place for Christ, because only
then are we in any sense ready to recognize and accept Christ as the totally
other, who is not me.

—RICHARD ROHR

DAY 29

What non-*Simple & Free*
meal are you most looking
forward to?

_____

_____

_____

_____

_____

_____

_____

_____

_____

_____

_____

_____

_____

_____

_____

DAY 30

What practice, idea, belief, or
rhythm from the past thirty
days do you want to keep with
you beyond this experiment?

MONTH TWO

CLOTHES

On any given day I wear jeans and a T-shirt. My style is utterly unsophisticated; I look like a college girl who rolled out of bed five minutes before class—but who has prematurely aged. Anyhow, I'm a simple or possibly lazy dresser who doesn't spend much time thinking about my wardrobe.

Clothes are just not a huge deal to me.

So, why clothes then? Why reduce radically in a neutral category I say I don't care about? Because although that sounds true in my head, my closet tells me a different story. I walked through all five of our closets, and I realized we spent real cash on every single item. I did some fuzzy averaging, and if we spent around ten dollars on each item, our closets represent an expenditure of, well, a lot of money. (I'm a writer, not an accountant.) It is such a high total I had to sit down. Especially considering we don't wear half of the items.

Underwear doesn't count. It just doesn't, okay? Between bra, panties, and socks, I'd use up half my allotment before I got my pants on. I considered omitting understuff from my wardrobe, but unleashing my free-swinging lady self onto this innocent world is probably a felony. No one deserves that kind of visual assault. So undergarments get a free pass, and if that makes me a *Simple & Free* slacker, well, at least I'm a slacker wearing a bra.

Here are my clothes for the month:

- One pair of jeans, dark wash, kind of plain
- One long-sleeved solid black T-shirt, fitted
- One short-sleeved black "Haiti relief" T-shirt with white print
- One short-sleeved gray "Mellow Johnny's Bike Shop" T-shirt with yellow print
- One pair of gray knit drawstring capri pants
- One long dark brown silk dress shirt
- Shoes: cowboy boots and tennis shoes

DAY 1

What are your seven pieces of clothing? What made you choose these pieces?

DAY 2

What does your relationship to clothes/fashion look like? Are you like me—more or less blasé about it all, yet somehow guilty of a bustling closet—or are you a deliberate lover of cultivating style?

_____

_____

_____

_____

_____

_____

_____

_____

_____

_____

_____

_____

_____

_____

_____

DAY 3

What do you think is, or will be,
the hardest part about paring
down options for clothes?

_____

_____

_____

_____

_____

_____

_____

_____

_____

_____

_____

_____

_____

_____

DAY 4

Maybe once we slow the cash hemorrhaging, some buried issues could surface, interrupting our default settings and raising questions we've never asked.

DAY 5

What upcoming events, people, or environments worry you when it comes to the thought of having only seven pieces of clothing? For me, it was a women's speaking event in Atlanta, where girls come out of the womb dressed to the nines.

DAY 6

_____

_____

_____

_____

_____

_____

_____

_____

_____

_____

_____

_____   In my first *Simple & Free*
                                          experiment with clothes, my
_____   friends and I organized a
                                          clothing swap to sustainably
_____   freshen up our wardrobes while
                                          resisting the consumer
_____   machine. What are some ways
                                          you can similarly pursue
_____   creativity and sustainability?

DAY 7

What's something you can celebrate about the past few weeks? It can have nothing to do with *Simple & Free*; it can have everything to do with *Simple & Free*. It can be a small win a friend had recently that you just want to pause and give attention to. What's that thing for you?

DAY 8

This next generation takes a lot of crap for being entitled or lazy, but let me tell you: they are a thousand times more sophisticated than we were when it comes to conservation, consumerism, and wastefulness. They care. They are paying attention to the planet and supply chains and their own carbon footprint. I have a ton of faith in them; I believe they'll do what our generation has been unwilling to do in order to rescue this groaning earth.

DAY 9

What are five things you love about this part of *Simple & Free*?

1.

2.

3.

4.

5.

DAY 10

What are five things you . . . don't love about this part of *Simple & Free?*

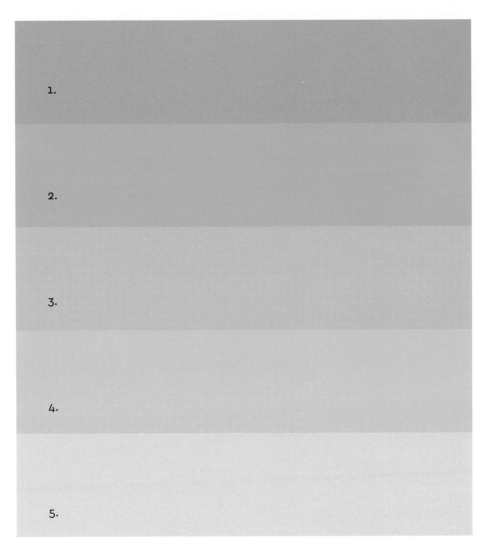

1.

2.

3.

4.

5.

DAY 11

_____

_____

_____

_____

_____

_____

_____

_____

_____

_____

_____

_____

Is there anything you've noticed
you think less about since the
start of this experiment? Is there
anything you've noticed you
think more about?

_____

_____

_____

Oh, how we love our religious yokes, not for what they communicate about God, but what they say about us. This is the kind of people we are. We say "no" when everyone else says "yes." We don't do <u>that</u>. We don't watch <u>that</u>. We don't vote <u>that</u> way. We don't go <u>there</u>. We don't include <u>them</u>.

But God's idea of a fast is less about what we're against and more about what we are <u>for</u>.

DAY 13

How has this experiment made
you look at clothes differently?

_____

_____

_____

_____

_____

_____

_____

_____

_____

_____

_____

_____

_____

_____

DAY 14

Who has been inspiring you and challenging you for good during this season? Could be a friend, a family member, or someone you follow on social. What do they do or say that moves you?

_____

_____

_____

_____

_____

_____

_____

_____

_____

_____

_____

_____

_____

_____

_____

_____

DAY 15

Think about your seven clothing pieces. What does each remind you of?

1.

2.

3.

4.

5.

6.

7.

When thirty-five years of choices overwhelm me, Jesus makes it simple again: "Love your neighbor as yourself." If you read the story, you'll see that Jesus takes a broad, global, interracial view of who our neighbor is.

DAY 17

_____

_____

_____

_____

_____

_____

_____

_____

_____

_____

_____

_____

When you buy clothes, what
are the factors that motivate
your thinking and spending
habits?

_____

_____

_____

DAY 18

What are some ways you can
implement more ethical,
thoughtful, and sustainable
consumer practices? (Once this
month is over, of course.)

DAY 19

Flip back to the first days of this journal. What do you know now that you didn't know then?

The average human gets around twenty-five thousand days on this earth, and most of us in the United States of America will get a few more. That's it. This life is a breath, and we live in that thin space where faith and obedience have relevance. We have this one life to offer; we get one shot at living to expand the kingdom, fighting for justice.

DAY 21

What's the hardest part of this
journey so far?

_____

_____

_____

_____

_____

_____

_____

_____

_____

_____

_____

_____

_____

_____

DAY 22

What have you become more
aware of in this experiment?

DAY 23

Look back to the first couple of days. Have you forgotten any parts of your initial reasons for starting this journey? Do you still resonate with those reasons?

Jesus didn't garner esteem the conventional way, but make no mistake: He was noticed. He was loved by the outsider, hated by the religious elite, revered by His followers, and killed by His enemies. For a plain carpenter from Nazareth, Jesus sure found His way to the center ring—not through power or ruthlessness but through subversion and truth. His humility appeals to the unloveliness in us all. We are drawn in by His simplicity, then transformed by His magnificence.

DAY 25

What are some parts of Jesus'
lifestyle that resonate with you?
What parts do you want to
emulate more?

_____

_____

_____

_____

_____

_____

_____

_____

_____

_____

_____

_____

_____

_____

_____

_____

_____

DAY 26

What pieces of art—whether it's a visual you caught in a museum, or a piece of writing from a book or article that struck you recently, or a chorus from a song that's been on heavy rotation lately—have been sustaining you?

DAY 27

Jesus' kingdom continues in the same manner it was launched: through humility, subversion, love, sacrifice; through calling empty religion to reform and behaving like we believe the meek will indeed inherit the earth. We cannot carry the gospel to the poor and lowly while emulating the practices of the rich and powerful. We've been invited into a story that begins with humility and ends with glory, never the other way around. Let's align ourselves correctly, sharing in the humble ministry of Jesus, knowing one day we'll feast at His table in splendor.

DAY 28

_____

_____

_____

_____

_____

_____

_____

_____

_____

_____

_____

_____

_____

_____

_____

_____

Has there been an emotion, a
result, or a revelation that has
surprised you so far?

DAY 29

What do you want to keep from
this part of the experiment?
What are you excited to return
to after this experiment?

_____

_____

_____

_____

_____

_____

_____

_____

_____

_____

_____

_____

_____

_____

_____

DAY 30

What has this month taught you about yourself?

_____

_____

_____

_____

_____

_____

_____

_____

_____

_____

_____

_____

_____

_____

_____

_____

MONTH THREE

POSSESSIONS

About three times a year, I rant around the house, screaming at our stuff: "What is all this? Why do we have so much junk? How am I supposed to keep up with all this? Where did this all come from?" And then I remember:

I bought it all.

I am starving for reform. Here is the deal:

One month.

Give seven things away that we own.

Every day.

Let's do this.

I had come to see that the great tragedy in the church is not that rich Christians do not care about the poor but that rich Christians do not know the poor. . . . I long for the Calcutta slums to meet the Chicago suburbs, for lepers to meet landowners and for each to see God's image in the other. . . . I truly believe that when the poor meet the rich, riches will have no meaning. And when the rich meet the poor, we will see poverty come to an end.

—SHANE CLAIBORNE

DAY 1

This month, use each day to document the seven things you choose to give away. On Day 1, what are the seven possessions you've given away, or are planning to give away? What do these seven things mean to you?

1.

2.

3.

4.

5.

6.

7.

DAY 2

What are your seven picks for today? What does each signify for you?

1.

2.

3.

4.

5.

6.

7.

DAY 3

What are your seven possessions you'll give away today? How did each of these wind up in your home?

1.

2.

3.

4.

5.

6.

7.

DAY 4

Think about the possessions you've given away so far. What common denominator do they share?

DAY 5

When you consider the items
you tend to identify to give
away, what season(s) of your life
do they represent for you?

_____

_____

_____

_____

_____

_____

_____

_____

_____

_____

_____

_____

_____

_____

_____

DAY 6

What will you miss about today's items?

1. _____

2. _____

3. _____

4. _____

5. _____

6. _____

7. _____

DAY 7

What makes you excited to get rid of today's possessions?

1.

2.

3.

4.

5.

6.

7.

DAY 8

Having thrown myself into this arena for a few months, I thought I would be thrilled to rip those boots off my rich feet and happily give them over to the homeless (who would promptly sell them since they are entirely impractical and worth a pretty penny—I've learned a few things). But I was discouraged to feel the twinge of selfishness rear its head first. Seriously? I'm going to make a deal over boots? Have I come only this far, God? I suck.

Jesus, unwilling to entertain my melodrama, cut to the chase: "Give them up. I have something to teach you."

DAY 9

What will you give away today?

1.

2.

3.

4.

5.

6.

7.

DAY 10

What conversations have you
had with friends, family, and/or
your community about this part
of the experiment?

DAY 11

What have you learned about
yourself through the past ten
days that you didn't realize
previously?

_____

_____

_____

_____

_____

_____

_____

_____

_____

_____

_____

_____

_____

_____

If we all raised others up instead of raising ourselves a little higher, there would be few needs left on earth. We each meet unique needs in our cities and our world. I marvel at what God accomplishes with the generosity of His sons and daughters. I'm proud they are brothers and sisters. What a family.

DAY 13

Are there certain categories of possessions that feel easier to let go of than others? E.g., pots and pans are easier to give away than are clothes. What does that look like for you?

DAY 14

What are you giving away today? What do you hope happens to these guys?

1.

2.

3.

4.

5.

6.

7.

DAY 15

Think about the reasons you
started this experiment in the
first place. Have they amplified
along the way, or shrunk back?
How have they evolved?

DAY 16

<u>Simple & Free</u> is becoming epically transformative. Tension led me here; now God is making a mess of things. I sense God preparing us for change. My sensitivity is peaking — noteworthy because I have the sensitivity of a thirteen-year-old boy. I feel raw and less and less attached to my stuff. Scripture is pouncing on my brain like a panther. It's like when I first got glasses and couldn't get over how clear everything was. And I walked weird because my perception was altered. I kept shouting, "Look at all the leaves! I can see every leaf on the tree!" like it was a miracle after having been impaired so long.

I have no idea what this means, but my hands are opening. I know my next phase of life is not going to look the same.

DAY 17

What do you miss about your
life before this part of the
experiment? What are you
looking forward to once this
part is over?

_____

_____

_____

_____

_____

_____

_____

_____

_____

_____

_____

_____

_____

_____

_____

_____

DAY 18

What are the seven things you're thinking about giving away today?

1.

2.

3.

4.

5.

6.

7.

DAY 19

Think back to the items you
mentioned a few days back—
the ones that you've been
thinking about but feel are hard
to lose. Where are they now?

_____

_____

_____

_____

_____

_____

_____

_____

_____

_____

_____

_____

_____

_____

DAY 20

We're just about to become adults, to honestly let the Gospel speak to us, to listen to what Jesus says, in no uncertain terms, about poverty and about leading a simple life in this world, a life that shows trust in God and not in our own power and weapons. God never promised us security in this world. God promised us only truth and freedom in our hearts. What does all this mean for us? It means that we're on the way.

—RICHARD ROHR

DAY 21

What are today's seven giveaways?

1.

2.

3.

4.

5.

6.

7.

DAY 22

Write out a prayer of thanks today.

DAY 23

Today, write a prayer that tells God what you need.

DAY 24

What if a bunch of Christians wrote a new story, becoming consumers the earth is groaning for? I suspect we'd find that elusive contentment, storing up treasures in heaven like Jesus told us to. I'm betting our stuff would lose its grip and we'd discover riches contained in a simpler life, a communal responsibility. Money is the most frequent theme in Scripture; perhaps the secret to happiness is right under our noses. Maybe we don't recognize satisfaction because it is disguised as radical generosity, a strange misnomer in a consumer culture.

How has the practice of giving
away affected your relationship
to your possessions in general?

_____

_____

_____

_____

_____

_____

_____

_____

_____

_____

_____

_____

_____

_____

DAY 26

What has been inspiring,
motivating, or energizing for
you during this experiment?

Today, I have a million and a half followers on social media. In every category of work, I make more money now. And yet the increase in fame and income did not shield me from loss, pain, trauma, or suffering. Nor did it make me categorically happier. It really didn't. The goodness of life is still located where it always was: in family, friends, memories, Jesus.

DAY 28

_____

_____

_____

_____

_____

_____

_____

_____

_____

_____

_____

_____

_____

_____

_____

_____   What do you want to take from
                                      this experiment, and keep as a
_____   rhythm in your life beyond the
                                      duration of the _Simple & Free_
_____   journey?

DAY 29

How has this experiment
shaped, influenced, or changed
the way you think about the
terms "treasures in heaven" and
"treasures on earth"?

_____

_____

_____

_____

_____

_____

_____

_____

_____

_____

_____

_____

_____

_____

_____

_____

DAY 30

A child says "me." An adult says "us." Maturity deciphers need from want, wisdom from foolishness. Growing up means curbing appetites, shifting from "me" to "we," understanding private choices have social consequences and public outcomes. Let's be consumers who silence the screaming voice that yells, "I WANT!" and instead listen to the quiet "we need," the marginalized voice of the worldwide community we belong to.

MONTH FOUR

MEDIA

This month, we stop the madness.

We're going radio silent. We're shutting down seven screens and muting the chatter. For instance, no

- TV
- Gaming
- Facebook/Twitter
- iPhone apps
- Radio
- Texting*
- Internet*

Asterisk 1: our texting rule: If it is a time-saver and/or necessary, then text away. If it's to be sarcastic, silly, or inappropriate, then pass. We're deferring to our own discernment, so someone should check my texts weekly because heaven knows I need accountability.

Asterisk 2: The Internet is a necessary tool for our jobs and life. Event planners, the kids' teachers, our adoption agency, my Restore Group, agent and publisher, and my neighbors correspond through e-mail. Additionally, I do research for my books and messages online. I can't ditch Internet for a month.

DAY 1

What are your seven media items for this fast?

1.

2.

3.

4.

5.

6.

7.

DAY 2

What worries you most about this particular experiment?

DAY 3

What excited you about this
experiment?

_____

_____

_____

_____

_____

_____

_____

_____

_____

_____

_____

_____

_____

_____

_____

Take something away,
and your habits
become clear.

DAY 5

_____

_____

_____

_____

_____

_____

_____

_____

_____

_____

_____

_____

In the absence of media and all
its noise, what has the silence
been like for you? Is it peaceful?
Unnerving? Welcome? Strange?

DAY 6

_____

_____

_____

What are some activities and
moments when you've found
yourself to be more present, in
the absence of media?

DAY 7

In the best world, where all dreams and hopes come true, what happens to/for you at the end of this experiment?

DAY 8

God is using <u>Simple & Free</u> to transform the ease of my communion with Him. It's intimacy like a comfortable sweatshirt, beyond dressed-up Sunday wear—past the formality, past the spiritual tasks. More like "Let's just live this life together." Something more relational and daily. Something in the gaps of spiritual activities, in between the stuff on a calendar. It's just simple communion, the natural kind between people who spend a lot of time together. I'm pondering this:

He has shown you, O mortal, what is good. And what does the Lord require of you? To act justly and to love mercy and to walk humbly with your God (Mic. 6:8).

God is teaching me <u>walk humbly</u>—daily, simply, quietly. If more of us took the "walk humbly with your God" part seriously, we might become agents of justice and mercy without even meaning to.

DAY 9

What do you miss about the media you've chosen for your fast?

DAY 10

What are the best and worst things about this experiment so far?

DAY 11

Have you digital-detoxed
before? What was that like? If
you haven't, what did you think
about the idea?

_____

_____

_____

_____

_____

_____

_____

_____

_____

_____

_____

_____

_____

_____

_____

_____

_____

DAY 12

What have you found yourself
craving during this experiment?

I'm just beginning to embrace the liberation that only exists at the bottom, where I have nothing to defend, nothing to protect. Where it doesn't matter if I'm right or esteemed or positioned well. I wonder if that's the freedom Jesus meant when He said, "Blessed are the poor in spirit, for theirs is the kingdom of heaven" (Matt. 5:3). In order for Jesus' kingdom to come, my kingdom will have to go, and for the first time I think I'm okay with that.

DAY 14

Who are the people in your corner who have been sustaining you during this journey? Write some words of gratitude to them.

DAY 15

What has this season of quiet,
of silence, of lessened noise
taught you about yourself?

_____

_____

_____

_____

_____

_____

_____

_____

_____

_____

_____

_____

_____

_____

_____

_____

_____

_____

DAY 16

I think each of us needs to ask, "What does it mean for a human being to flourish?" These technologies are forcing us to be more deliberate about asking that question. We need to sit down with ourselves and say, "As I look at my daily life, as I look at the past year, as I look at the past five years, what are the aspects of my life that have been the most rewarding and enriching? When have I been happiest? What are the things that have made me flourish?" If we ask these questions in a thoughtful, explicit way, then we can say more definitely what these technologies are adding to the human experience and, more importantly, what they're subtracting from the human experience.

—MICHAEL BESS

DAY 17

What is something you've
learned about modern life in the
past two weeks?

_____

_____

_____

_____

_____

_____

_____

_____

_____

_____

_____

_____

_____

_____

_____

_____

DAY 18

_____

_____

_____

_____

_____

_____

_____

_____

_____

_____

_____

_____

_____

_____

_____

_____

_____

_____

How has this particular fast
shaped your spiritual life?

DAY 19

Before this experiment, how did it feel whenever you consciously unplugged from media and devices? Has the continuity of this round made the experience feel different from those previous instances?

DAY 20

What element of media do you find yourself hungering for the most? Is it the company of some audible voices? Is it the storytelling? Is it background noise?

DAY 21

Who are some people who
have been inspiring you during
this journey? What are some
things they've said that have
energized you?

_____

_____

_____

_____

_____

_____

_____

_____

_____

_____

_____

_____

_____

DAY 22

_____

_____

_____

When you tell others about this
part of the experiment, what
language do you use to
describe it?

_____

_____

_____

_____

_____

_____

_____

_____

_____

_____

_____

DAY 23

What have your motivations looked like, specifically for this part of the experiment?

While I find a "good old days" approach overly sentimental and impractical, as technology is here to stay and an asset to global progress by any account, old-fashioned human contact cannot be replaced. Unplugged mental rest cannot be replaced. Experiencing the world through our senses cannot be replaced. We must be the grownups in the room; our technology cannot parent and rule us, or our kids.

DAY 25

What are some gifts that this
experiment has given you? They
could be time, silence, quiet—
one could even be discomfort.
What are some things that have
arisen?

_____

_____

_____

_____

_____

_____

_____

_____

_____

_____

_____

_____

_____

_____

_____

DAY 26

All right, be honest: What specific device or media outlet are you most looking forward to getting back?

DAY 27

It is possible to delete apps from our phones. We can declare entire days or time slots screen-free. We can charge phones overnight in another room in the house. We can limit our children's usage no matter what their peers say or do. This will all be increasingly countercultural, I'm afraid, but it is our responsibility to keep ourselves and families connected to each other, to other people, and to this gorgeous earth.

DAY 28

What's something you're
excited about not continuing
once this part of the experiment
is finished? What's something
you do want to continue?

DAY 29

Are there any other media forms you'd consider giving up?

DAY 30

How are you feeling today?

Let's review the months so far:

I ate Ethiopian food on the fifth day of *Simple & Free*.

I wore a nonsanctioned jacket during Day 1 of the clothes fast.

I pre-hoarded piles of clothes for giveaway month, just in case.

I came *this close* to watching TV during media fast.

I warned you about these tendencies. I never pretended I had a will of iron, people. That I'm still doing this is a miracle.

Let's keep going.

MONTH FIVE

WASTE

This month the Hatmakers are doing their part, setting aside apathy and respecting the earth God made and loves, trying to care for it in a way that makes sense for our kids and their kids and everyone's kids. Because let me tell you something: We are wasters. We are consumers. We are definitely a part of the problem. I no more think about how my consumption affects the earth or anyone else living on it than I think about becoming a personal trainer; there is just no category for it in my mind. (Please revisit my introduction to *Simple & Free,* where I declared repentance the first motivation. Thank you.)

So, Month Five—seven habits for a greener life, a fast from assuming I am not a part of an integrated earth but somehow above it all, expecting that sacrifices necessary to accommodate humanity should be made by species other than me. Sample habits to take up this month:

- Gardening
- Composting
- Conserving energy and water
- Recycling (everything, all of it)
- Driving only one car (for love of the land)
- Shopping thrift and secondhand
- Buying only local

DAY 1

What are the seven habits you're leaning into for a greener life?

1.

2.

3.

4.

5.

6.

7.

DAY 2

_____

_____

Have you tried any of these
habits/practices before? How
did that go?

_____

_____

_____

_____

_____

_____

_____

_____

_____

_____

_____

_____

_____

DAY 3

_____

_____

_____

_____

_____

_____

_____

_____

_____

_____

_____

_____

_____

_____

What's been the hardest
practice so far? What has that
been like?

_____

_____

DAY 4

The ecological teaching of the Bible is simply inescapable: God made the world because He wanted it made. He thinks the world is good, and He loves it. It is His world; He has never relinquished title to it. And He has never revoked the conditions, bearing on His gift to us of the use of it, that oblige us to take excellent care of it. If God loves the world, then how might any person of faith be excused for not loving it or justified in destroying it?

—WENDELL BERRY

DAY 5

What's one thing you love about yourself?

DAY 6

What are you learning to own about yourself?

DAY 7

What has this practice taught
you so far?

_____

_____

_____

_____

_____

_____

_____

_____

_____

_____

_____

_____

_____

_____

_____

_____

DAY 8

_____

_____

_____

_____

_____

_____

_____

_____

_____

_____

_____

_____

_____

_____

_____

_____

What aspect of yourself are you
trying to learn more about?

DAY 9

I keep thinking about our obsession with health. Our kids have been immunized, checked, prodded, measured, tested, and examined since the day they were born.

Why?

Because God gave us spectacular bodies, and we value them.

But as certainly as God created man in His image, He first created the earth. With the same care He designed sixty thousand miles of blood vessels in the human body, He also crafted hydrangeas and freshwater rapids and hummingbirds. He balanced healthy ecosystems with precision and established climates and beauty. He integrated colors and smells and sounds that would astound humanity. The details He included while designing the earth are so extraordinary, it is no wonder He spent five of the six days of creation on it.

DAY 10

Think of one person who's with
you on this journey—whether
by joining you in these
practices or by cheering you on
from afar. What's your favorite
thing about this person?

DAY 11

What is your relationship to the earth like? How has that changed since your childhood?

DAY 12

When does it feel hard to love others?

DAY 13

What's one small way you can create joy for yourself this week?

DAY 14

Why don't we care for the earth anywhere near to the degree we do our bodies? Why don't we fuss and examine and steward creation with the same tenacity? Why aren't we refusing complicity in the ravaging of our planet? Why aren't we determined to stop pillaging the earth's resources like savages? Why do we mock environmentalists and undermine their passion for conservation? Do we think ourselves so superior to the rest of creation that we are willing to deplete the earth to supply our luxuries? If so, we may very well be the last generation who gets that prerogative.

DAY 15

What's one small way you can create joy for a friend this week?

DAY 16

Between this month's practices,
and the past months of taking
stock of our consumption habits
at large, what big things are
you noticing about yourself—be
they habits, desires, tendencies,
or even the things you've
realized are easier than you
previously thought?

DAY 17

What's one thing you've picked up in the *Simple & Free* experiment so far that you want to keep practicing, thinking, believing, or doing long after this experiment concludes?

DAY 18

My hypocrisies are too numerous to count, but this month birthed something unmistakable: I'm done separating ecology from theology, pretending they don't originate from the same source.

DAY 19

Which habit, of the seven green practices this month, is the easiest so far? Which habit has been the hardest?

DAY 20

What's been fun for you
this week?

DAY 21

What are you looking
forward to?

DAY 22

What book, audiobook, podcast, or other piece of storytelling have you been enjoying recently?

_____

_____

_____

_____

_____

_____

_____

_____

_____

_____

_____

_____

_____

_____

DAY 23

The earth is the Lord's, and everything
    in it,
the world, and all who live in it;
for he founded it on the seas
and established it on the waters.

—Ps. 24:1–2

DAY 24

What has been sustaining you in these past few weeks of fasting and reducing? (You can be honest and say you've been barely hanging on by a thread here.)

_____

_____

_____

_____

_____

_____

_____

_____

_____

_____

_____

_____

_____

_____

_____

_____

DAY 25

_____

_____

_____

_____

_____

_____

_____

_____

_____

_____

_____

What's your favorite thing to
buy locally? What do you love
about it?

_____

_____

_____

DAY 26

In the past month or so, what are some things you've learned about waste and consumption at large? It could be something you've learned through practice, through personal trial and error, or through the news.

DAY 27

What's one current reality of our world that is sadly true? What's one thing you wish to be a current reality of our world?

You must take action. You must do

the impossible. Because giving up

can never ever be an option.

—GRETA THUNBERG

DAY 28

What will you take from this
practice onward?

DAY 29

What's been heavy on your
mind/heart lately?

_____

_____

_____

_____

_____

_____

_____

_____

_____

_____

_____

_____

_____

_____

_____

DAY 30

What do you want to see happen in the world in the next five years?

I am recommitting to doing the right thing. I am examining it all: our meat consumption, carbon footprint, waste, single-use products, travel, sourcing. I want to have an answer for my grandchildren when they ask what I did to reverse global warming. It is not too late. But this will be our generation's legacy... one way or another.

MONTH SIX

SPENDING

We're spending money in only seven places this month—a slight decrease in consuming (sarcasm): 89 percent fewer vendors in a month, for the love of Moses. These are the vendors getting our dough:

• Sunset Valley Farmers' Market
• H-E-B gas station (flex fuel!)
• Online bill pay
• Kids' school
• Limited travel fund
• Emergency medical
• Target

This means no restaurants, movie theaters, Chick-fil-A, no Coke and nachos at the UT/UCLA game (or parking), no Kindle/Barnes & Noble/amazon.com/Half Price Books to feed my habit, no lunch after church, no Hays High School football games unless my mom the Principal scores us free tickets, no hunting paraphernalia (Brandon), *Call of Duty 4* (Gavin), iTunes (Sydney), fishing worms (Caleb), and Mama Fu's spicy Mongolian beef over brown rice with a beef curry roll (moi).

DAY 1

What are the seven places you'll allow yourself to spend this month? Name one thing you love or can't live without from each place.

1.

2.

3.

4.

5.

6.

7.

DAY 2

_____

_____

What practices and progresses
would you like to see in your
spending and giving habits?

_____

_____

_____

_____

_____

_____

_____

_____

_____

_____

_____

_____

_____

_____

DAY 3

Is there something you've
always wanted to do, that you
feel more empowered to do
given the practices this month?

_____

_____

_____

_____

_____

_____

_____

_____

_____

_____

_____

_____

_____

_____

DAY 4

And when I get a teeny bit discouraged that my little rage against the machine is silly, I remember that I'm making healthier choices for my family and rediscovering the farm-to-table system God created, and that counts. When I look at the resources of our earth and all the humans it needs to sustain, I have to adopt an "as for me and my house" perspective on responsibility.

DAY 5

What have you noticed about yourself, your lifestyle, or your community's habits that you hadn't noticed previously?

DAY 6

What has informed the spirituality of ecology in your life?

DAY 7

_____

_____

_____

_____

_____

_____

_____

_____

_____

_____

_____

_____

What are ways you've pursued
simplicity and reduced
spending and consumerism in
the past?

_____

_____

_____

DAY 8

The earth is groaning, and
we're putting coffee bars in our
$35 million sanctuaries. Just
because we can have it doesn't
mean we should. I marvel at
how out of place simple, humble
Jesus would be in today's
American churches.

DAY 9

What feels hard about living the
kind of simple, humble lifestyle
Jesus demonstrated?

_____

_____

_____

_____

_____

_____

_____

_____

_____

_____

_____

_____

_____

_____

_____

It takes true courage to rage against this machine. Could we be countercultural enough to say, "We're not buying that. We don't need that. We'll make do with what we have. We'll use the stuff we already own"? If this causes anxiety, I'm with you, trust me. Because who else does that?

But we can—we can stop spending so much; use what we have, borrow what we need, repurpose possessions instead of replacing them; and—the kicker—live with less.

DAY 11

What has been giving you hope lately?

_____

_____

_____

_____

_____

_____

_____

_____

_____

_____

_____

_____

_____

_____

_____

DAY 12

"You're hopeless, you Pharisees! Frauds! You keep meticulous account books, tithing on every nickel and dime you get, but manage to find loopholes for getting around basic matters of justice and God's love. Careful bookkeeping is commendable, but the basics are required."

—LUKE 11:42, THE MESSAGE

DAY 13

_____

_____

_____

_____

_____

_____

_____

_____

_____

_____

_____

How have your original
motivations for engaging in the
Simple & Free experiment
changed, evolved, reshaped, or
remained in the past few
months?

_____

_____

_____

_____

DAY 14

How have you surprised yourself in this journey?

DAY 15

Think of someone in your corner. Write a thank-you card to them here.

I'm starting to wonder if Jesus actually meant what He said. Was He serious about sanctification through extreme generosity? Is He really advocating redistribution? I don't know if He knows this, but this would mean completely retooling the way we live and spend.

DAY 17

What has surprised you about
Jesus in your reflections on
Him?

_____

_____

_____

_____

_____

_____

_____

_____

_____

_____

_____

_____

_____

_____

_____

_____

_____

_____

DAY 18

Do you view faith, spirituality,
church, or Jesus differently than
you did when you first started?
In what ways?

_____

_____

_____

_____

_____

_____

_____

_____

_____

_____

_____

_____

_____

_____

DAY 19

What's been bringing you joy recently?

_____

_____

_____

_____

_____

_____

_____

_____

_____

_____

_____

_____

_____

_____

_____

DAY 20

What if we're buying a bag of tricks? What if wealth and indulgence are creating a polished people rotting from the inside out, without even knowing it? Is there a reason Jesus called the rich blind, deaf, unseeing, unhearing, and foolish? Jesus never utters a positive word about the wealthy, only tons of parables with us as the punch line and this observation: It is terribly hard for us to receive His kingdom, harder than shoving a camel through the eye of a needle. <u>That's really hard.</u> If this is true, then more than fearing poverty or simplicity, we should fear prosperity.

DAY 21

What is your relationship to money like? How has it changed—or remained—in the past few years?

DAY 22

What person, truth, affirmation, or prayer is sustaining you lately?

DAY 23

What's the best thing that happened to you in the past week?

DAY 24

Your love, Lord, reaches to the
heavens,
your faithfulness to the skies.

Your righteousness is like the highest
mountains,
your justice like the great deep.
You, Lord, preserve both people and
animals.

How priceless is your unfailing love,
O God!
People take refuge in the shadow of
your wings.

They feast on the abundance of your
house;
you give them drink from your river of
delights.

For with you is the fountain of life;
in your light we see light.

—Ps. 36:5–9

DAY 25

What are you most looking
forward to once this fast is
over?

_____

_____

_____

_____

_____

_____

_____

_____

_____

_____

_____

_____

_____

_____

_____

_____

DAY 26

Throughout the anniversary edition, I write notes to myself—myself from ten years ago. What would you say to yourself from ten years back?

DAY 27

At some point, the church stopped living the Bible and decided just to study it, culling the feast parts and whitewashing the fast parts. We are addicted to the buffet, skillfully discarding the costly discipleship required after consuming. <u>The feast is supposed to sustain the fast,</u> but we go back for seconds and thirds and fourths, stuffed to the brim and fat with inactivity. All this is for me.

Not so with members of the early church, who stunned their Roman neighbors and leaders with generosity, curbing their own appetites for the mission of Jesus. They constantly practiced self-denial to alleviate human misery.

DAY 28

What will you miss about this month? What won't you miss?

DAY 29

What's one thing you've learned about yourself from the past few months of these fasts?

DAY 30

What was your greatest joy and challenge this month?

MONTH SEVEN

STRESS

For the love of Barnum and Bailey, we have too much going on. We are short-fused, stressed out, overextended, and unrested. This pace is not sustainable. I don't want it to be. This season of life is passing me by, accelerated by a lack of boundaries. Most days I just try to keep the wheels on, not living in the moment at all; I'm just getting it done while thinking about what's left. My kids and husband get half answers, and eye contact is a crapshoot. Every day I could take a two-hour nap, so exhausted do I feel at 1:00 P.M. I have considered abandoning my career over the volume of e-mails.

Such is the ridiculous American life. Every one of my friends has a similar story. None of us are happy about it, yet we keep filling the calendars. Yes, I'm in; we'll sign up; I'll do it. We race from one activity to another, teaching our children to max out and stress out. Nice legacy.

After six months of *Simple & Free,* I am ready to tackle resting and prayer. On the seventh day God rested, and in the seventh month we will too. The kids are thrilled, instinctively understanding that fasting from a fast life has "marvelous" written all over it. Plus, it won't mess with their Game Boys or access to Double Dave's Pizzaworks for the Wednesday buffet.

For Month Seven, our guide will be *Seven Sacred Pauses,* written by Macrina Wiederkehr, member of the monastic community St. Scholastica, whose wisdom is so profound, I underlined nearly every sentence in the book. She quotes Pius Parsch, who describes the pauses as "breathing spells for the soul," oases to remember the sacredness of life, who we are, how to offer God the incredible gift of our lives, and learn to *be* in the midst of so much doing. We will pause and pray seven times a day:

> The Night Watch (midnight)
> The Awakening Hour (dawn)
> The Blessing Hour (midmorning)
> The Hour of Illumination (noon)
> The Wisdom Hour (midafternoon)
> The Twilight Hour (early evening)
> The Great Silence (bedtime)

DAY 1

What pauses will you embed in your daily rhythm this month?

1.

2.

3.

4.

5.

6.

7.

DAY 2

What do you anticipate will be hard about these practices? What are you looking forward to?

DAY 3

What practices of silence, contemplation, rest, or pause have you exercised in the past?

_____

_____

_____

_____

_____

_____

_____

_____

_____

_____

_____

_____

_____

_____

_____

_____

DAY 4

Put your hope in God,
for I will yet praise him,
my Savior and my God.

—Ps. 42:11

(Thanks for being
hope! God, I want to
be hope too. And I pray
these forgotten, lonely,
and abandoned people
will not give up hope.)

DAY 5

What readings have been
sustaining you?

DAY 6

_____

_____

_____

What do you savor about
these silences? What's been
uncomfortable about them?

_____

_____

_____

_____

_____

_____

_____

_____

_____

_____

_____

_____

DAY 7

_____

_____

_____

_____

_____

_____

_____

_____

_____

_____

_____

What Sabbath fails have you encountered so far? No judgment—in the _Simple & Free_ book, clearly I have no shortage of these guys.

_____

_____

_____

DAY 8

_____

_____

_____

_____

_____

_____

_____

_____

_____

_____

_____

_____

_____

_____

_____

_____

_____

Which Sabbath exercise has
been your favorite so far?

DAY 9

There remains, then, a Sabbath-rest
for the people of God; for anyone who
enters God's rest also rests from their
works, just as God did from his. Let us,
therefore, make every effort to enter
that rest, so that no one will perish by
following their example of disobedi-
ence.

—HEB. 4:9–11

DAY 10

What do you do to replenish and reenergize yourself?

_____

_____

_____

_____

_____

_____

_____

_____

_____

_____

_____

_____

_____

_____

_____

_____

_____

_____

DAY 11

What are some activities you do to rest and wind down?

DAY 12

Who are safe people who help you recuperate?

Maybe Sabbath isn't just another spiritual task to wear us out. Perhaps God designed this as a gift, not an obligation. What if God understood our tendency to overwork and underrest, so He made it mandatory for believers to breathe . . . pause . . . pray . . . relax every week? Maybe Jesus meant it when He said, "The Sabbath was made for man, not man for the Sabbath" (Mark 2:27). God ordained the Sabbath for us, not as just another requirement from us.

DAY 14

What has been weighing you
down lately that you want to
hand over to the Lord?

DAY 15

What meals, foods, drinks, or other goodies do you associate with Sabbath rest?

DAY 16

Who in your life do you notice observing Sabbath in a really beautiful way?

This month, we follow the
ancients, the monastics, and
the contemplatives into the
practice of honoring the hours.
Those humble enough to pause
and touch the grace of the
hour have hallowed these
rhythms for centuries.

DAY 18

We're a little over halfway
through this month where we
fast from stress. What has this
time revealed to you?

DAY 19

What do you feel generates the
most stress in your life?

_____

_____

_____

_____

_____

_____

_____

_____

_____

_____

_____

_____

_____

_____

_____

_____

_____

DAY 20

_____

_____

_____

_____

_____

_____

_____

_____

_____

_____

_____

_____

_____

_____

_____

_____

_____

_____

How has your relationship with
silence remained, evolved, or
changed so far?

_____

DAY 21

Satisfy us in the morning with
your unfailing love;
so that we may sing for joy
and be glad all our days.

—Ps. 90:14

DAY 22

Reader, let's pause and consider what a feat it is that you've made it this far into the journey. Whether you stuck to this experiment hard-core, all day, every day for seven months straight, or you hopped on/hopped off, or somewhere in between the two, thank you for joining me. How are you feeling today?

_____

_____

_____

_____

_____

_____

_____

_____

_____

_____

_____

_____

_____

_____

_____

_____

DAY 23

What has this experiment of fasting from stress shown you about your desires? Do you crave business, rest, activity?

DAY 24

Which of your seven pauses do you find yourself most looking forward to?

DAY 25

O You whose face is a thousand colors . . . look upon us in this twilight hour, and color our faces with the radiance of your love. As the light of the sun fades away, light the lamps of our hearts that we may see one another more clearly.

—MACRINA WIEDERKEHR

DAY 26

As this seven-month experiment comes to a slow close, which month was your favorite, and why?

_____

_____

_____

_____

_____

_____

_____

_____

_____

_____

_____

_____

_____

_____

_____

_____

_____

_____

_____

_____

_____

_____

DAY 27

_____

_____

_____

_____

_____

_____

_____

_____

_____

_____

_____

_____

Which part of the *Simple & Free*
experiment do you want to try
again?

_____

_____

_____

The Sabbath is holy.
Not lazy, not selfish,
not unproductive;
not helpful, not optional,
not just a good idea.
Holy.

DAY 29

What were the hardest
challenges from this month?

_____

_____

_____

_____

_____

_____

_____

_____

_____

_____

_____

_____

_____

_____

DAY 30

What were the greatest joys
from this month?

What happens in the spiritual realm when we pray? It's such a mystery. What words prompt the Spirit to move? What goodness do we join Him on when we pray for peace?

How powerful are our prayer words? They are a catalyst for miracles, the impetus for healing. Does God wait for us to pray in His will, primed to move for righteousness?

How many relationships is He waiting to mend? How much turmoil is He poised to soothe? How much peace is He ready to administer? Are we withholding the necessary words to trigger God's intervention?

Perhaps this is why He urges us to forgive, release, lie down, let go, trust, offer, submit, and obey; these are the keys that turn the locks that bind.

CONCLUSION

This experimental mutiny against excess showed me that God and people matter. That's basically it. Everything else disintegrates when you clutch it too tightly. We have around one minute on this planet before our time is up, and this is our shot to build a more equitable world. It is our responsibility to challenge structures and systems that keep people out and down, locked in suffering while the same few prosper. This is our work. We are able in Jesus. His kingdom will come. His will done. May it be on earth as it is in heaven.